I0017588

THE BEST PLAN GAMING PC 2023

PC 2023

Best Financial plan Gaming PC 2023

CARLO DEMAND

Table of Contents

CHAPTER ONE

INTRODUCTION

PC Gaming could appear to be restrictively costly to get into, however financial plan gaming laptops offer a shockingly reasonable way into the side interest. You don't need to spend a full (or several) month's compensation to manage the cost of a gaming PC to play the best computer games. You can undoubtedly get a fit apparatus with a brand new computer chip and illustrations card for a great or less.

A reasonable apparatus is all you really want to help you through the PC gaming entryway to play AAA and independent games. You could get an apparatus with a little SSD or just a single stick of Smash, yet you can undoubtedly redesign or supplant these parts down the line. The equivalent goes with your gaming experience, to move up to a 4K gaming screen you can constantly purchase an all the more impressive GPU later on.

The Best Financial plan Gaming computers

The Lenovo Army 5i Pinnacle Gen 7 may be a tick more than $1,000; however the little added cost is definitely justified for Intel's twelfth Age Center i7 processor. That

12-center computer chip gives this gaming PC a lot of additional handling headroom and superb effectiveness when you're not gaming. Moreover, you get a lot of quick, upgradeable DDR5 memory, while the Nvidia RTX 3060 designs installed will see you through a lot of 1080p gaming.

One more incredible thing about the Lenovo Army 5i

Pinnacle Gen 7 is it's simply a fabulous gaming PC fabricate by and large. There are two front admission fans behind a lattice exterior and an exhaust fan at the back. Inside, it likewise includes a standard miniature ATX motherboard and a sizeable heatsink to keep your central processor cool. Furthermore, you get a PCIe 4.0 SSD, despite the fact that the drive is on the more modest side with a 256GB limit with respect to fast loads, while an extra 1TB HDD is helpful for additional capacity.

CHAPTER TWO

HP SIGN 25L GAMING WORK AREA

The HP Sign 25L Gaming Work area is an incredible gaming PC in the event that you have a hard spending plan breaking point of $1,000. It packs a twelfth gen Intel Center i5-12400 processor, which is an incredible midrange gaming computer chip with six P-centers and 12 strings that can overclock like it's no one's business. You'll have no issue cruising through ordinary undertakings, and it's a gaming workhorse. Obviously, matching that processor with Nvidia RTX 3050 designs makes this machine a 1080p gaming champion, however if you need to game at higher goals, it'll cost you the casing rate.

This gaming PC isn't exactly unlimited, with just DDR4 Smash and a PCIe 3.0 SSD, yet you have all that you want to begin playing computer games with 8GB of memory and 256GB of extra room. In the event that that doesn't seem sufficiently like, the HP Sign 25L offers a lot of custom updates you can make while buying, or it carries a really enormous PC case, so you can undoubtedly trade your parts later on.

HP Victus 15L

At a cost south of $700, the HP Victus 15L is one of indisputably the least expensive computers for gaming accessible that is really worth purchasing. The AMD Ryzen 5 5600G is an incredibly strong computer processor, and, surprisingly, the low-power AMD Radeon RX 6400 conveys an astonishing measure of graphical snort. You ought to accomplish around 60fps gaming on AAA titles at a 1080p goal and your visual quality set to high, which isn't excessively ratty while thinking about the cost.

The HP Victus 15L is a minuscule apparatus, so it's ideal in the event that you likewise don't have a lot of room for a work area. It even offers a touch of RGB lighting in the front board for that gamer stylish, while nine USB ports are accessible to connect every one of your peripherals. The main disadvantage is it accompanies a pattern of 8GB of memory and 256GB of stockpiling, however that is all you really want to begin messing around, and you can continuously overhaul not too far off.

CyberPowerPC Gamer Xtreme Gaming Work area

1440p gaming could appear to be incomprehensible on a careful spending plan, however the CyberPowerPC Gamer Xtreme is an incredible, but restricted, bargain at just shy of $1,500. It's completely stacked with the most recent Intel Center i5-13600KF processor, which offers 14 centers and exceptional single-strung execution ideal for games. At the point when you pair that with the Nvidia RTX 3060 Ti designs, you prepare a machine to make your QHD and beam followed gaming dreams a reality — and it's able to do some high FPS in 1080p gaming when you're in that frame of mind.

Advancing along that amazing degree of execution is 16GB of DDR4 memory to keep everything moving along as expected, even while performing various tasks with illustrations weighty projects, and 1TB of SSD stockpiling guarantees your games boot up rapidly. To hold that multitude of strong parts back from overheating, the CyberPowerPC Gamer Xtreme has a ventilated case and a fluid cooling framework set up. It likewise accompanies a gaming console and mouse, adding to the PC's worth, while eight USB ports and two DisplayPorts mean you can connect a lot of different peripherals.

NZXT Streaming PC

If you would rather not penance outline rates, 1080p is the best approach while gaming on a careful spending plan, and the NZXT Streaming PC offers heavenly execution at that goal at a fair cost. Carrying a fit Nvidia

RTX 3060 designs card, you can appreciate messing around at a velvety 1080p with the most noteworthy settings. It'll try and deal with a touch of gaming at 1440p, however not close to as well as the Corsair Retaliation a7200. That GPU coordinates impeccably with the midrange AMD Ryzen 5 5600X processor to bite through most games easily.

Past its processors, the NZXT Streaming PC additionally accompanies 16GB of memory and 1TB of fast SSD stockpiling, which is a lot for anybody simply beginning in the PC gaming space or easygoing gamers. Obviously, the "streaming" in the name likewise involves a smooth stream over Jerk while you play and a lot of ports for every one of your peripherals. Furthermore, to guarantee every one of the PC's parts keep up top execution, a strong fluid cooler with some RGB lighting is incorporated, while the large case gives more than adequate space to part trading.

CHAPTER THREE

What to Search for in a Spending plan Gaming PC

The best gaming laptops will perpetually be expensive, particularly in the event that you intend to play graphically-serious games at high or ultra settings, yet finding a respectable and reasonable gaming rig isn't unimaginable.

Simply accept our picks above for instance; it's not difficult to imagine tracking down work areas to assist you with beginning with PC gaming without spending more than $1,000. The main thing is you really want to find designs with a sufficient processor and illustrations cards to address your issues. We'll separate what to search for on a for every part premise.

Discrete GPU

Because of the restored contest among AMD and Nvidia (and Intel soon), designs cards have never been all the more remarkable and reasonable. The drawback to this is that there are a ton of choices out there, and it can get pretty overpowering to pick when you're curious about them.

On the financial plan range, the Nvidia RTX 3060 has turned into the defacto designs card for the vast majority. Obviously, you can shoot a little lower with the Nvidia a tad more reserve funds, however this GPU is best for serious like CS:GO and Class of Legends.

Concerning AMD, the AMD Radeon RX 6600 XT and AMD Radeon RX 6700 XT — or their new marginally

refreshed replacements —
frequently accompany even
lower-evaluated rigs. In the
event that you're searching
for something low priced, the
AMD Radeon RX 6500 XT is a
strong scratch and dent
section entertainer.

Processor

The second thing you ought
to consider about your
gaming PC is the processor.
While the central processor
doesn't straightforwardly

drive how your games will look, they truly do decide how well they will run.

Having the most recent processor is less significant than having the most recent designs cards, notwithstanding, Intel's twelfth Age and AMD's fifth Era computer chips address the biggest computer processor upgrades we've found in years past. So it merits searching out the most current chips you can find in the event that you can bear the cost of them.

So, you ought to in a perfect world track down a gaming PC with either an Intel Center i5-12400 or AMD Ryzen 5 5600X. While looking for a financial plan gaming PC you likewise could likewise run over designs with an AMD Ryzen 5 5600G or Ryzen 7 5700G. These are basically AMD's APUs that offer incredible exhibition, astounding incorporated designs, and frequently additional investment funds, so there's no great explanation to stay away from choices with these computer processors.

Slam

The speed and measure of Slam you have in your gaming PC is the third most significant element. In any event you need to have at least 8GB of DDR4 Slam, however most gaming laptops nowadays accompany somewhere around 16GB of memory. Likewise remember that it's normally less expensive to update your Slam then to do it at look at, so you could find it more prudent to pick a design with less memory and purchase a different pack to introduce.

CHAPTER FOUR

THE BEST MODEST GAMING PC

The best modest gaming PC is the HP Sign 40L on the grounds that it includes a magnificent central processor and GPU, alongside plentiful USB ports and update choices. It upholds Wi-Fi 6 for very quick paces and highlights RGB lighting that can be modified to flaunt your style.

Modest gaming PC

Cost

Computer chip

GPU

HP Sign 40L

$1100

Intel Center i5-12400F

Nvidia GeForce RTX 3060

HP Structure

$722

AMD Ryzen 5 5600G

AMD Radeon RX 5500

MSI Aegis R

$1080

Intel Center i5-12400F

Nvidia GeForce RTX 3050

Lenovo Army Pinnacle 5i Gen 7

$1255

Intel Center i7-12700

Nvidia GeForce RTX 3060

HP Victus Pinnacle

$390

Intel Center i3-12100F

Nvidia GeForce GTX 1650

Which financial plan gaming PC is appropriate for you?

Whenever you've settled your spending plan, you'll need to pick a gaming PC that has sufficient extra room for a little library of your #1 games as well as a lot of Smash for smooth interactivity. You'll likewise need to ensure that the included GPU is adequately strong to deal with most famous games, and that the power supply can stay aware of your requirements as you trade out parts or add things like auxiliary stockpiling drives or more Slam sticks.

Pick this modest gaming PC...

Assuming you want...

HP Sign 40L

A balanced and financial plan accommodating gaming PC. It includes a twelfth gen Intel Center i5 computer chip and RTX 3060 designs card.

HP Structure

A spending plan AMD-based gaming PC. It's worked with an AMD Ryzen 5 5600G computer chip and Radeon RX 5500 designs card for lots of force for AMD supporters.

MSI Aegis R

A spending plan Intel-based gaming PC. It flaunts a twelfth gen Intel Center i5 processor and RTX 3050 illustrations card, making it simple to get top-quality parts without burning through every last dollar.

Lenovo Army Pinnacle 5i Gen 7

A gaming PC under $1500. This gaming PC retails for

about $1200 while as yet offering extraordinary elements like a RTX 3060 designs card and double stockpiling drives.

HP Victus Pinnacle

An ultra financial plan accommodating gaming PC. In the event that your financial plan is so close it squeaks, the HP Victus can be yours for under $500.

Alongside the value, I saw PC assembles that can deal with well known games like Fortnite, Zenith Legends, and Overwatch while additionally giving a lot of capacity to downloads, photographs, and recordings. I likewise picked constructs that can be arranged on the brand site, so anybody with adaptability in their spending plan can make their optimal gaming PC.

What would it be a good idea for me to search for in a gaming PC?

Regardless of what gaming PC you pick, ensure the item has a decent processor, an extraordinary GPU, and a nice cooling framework.

Is it better to purchase or fabricate a gaming PC?

While you can discover some reasonable prebuilt gaming laptops, you can likewise save yourself a smidgen more money by building your own PC. By building your own, you can exploit deals and arrangements on parts to get the greatest aspects at the least expensive costs. The compromise is getting some margin to assemble everything yourself, so you'll need to choose if you're agreeable enough structure your own PC, and whether you have the opportunity and energy to do as such.

Is a PC less expensive than a gaming PC?

Sadly, a PC intended for gaming will cost in excess of a PC tower. They utilize similar processors and designs cards, which add to the expense, as well as choices can imagine OLED or 4K touch screens, which are troublesome and costly to deliver - - the last cost of the

PC will mirror that. There are some extraordinary financial plan gaming PCs assuming that is the thing you're searching for, however they will not be a lot less expensive than a customary PC tower.

What is a decent financial plan for a gaming PC?

Indeed, even before the chip deficiencies, you were unable to find that numerous prebuilt gaming computers under $1,000. Presently, with GPUs increasingly hard to get a hold of, a prebuilt PC is about the best way to get your hands on one, much more seasoned ones like the GTX 1660 Super. Furthermore, they certainly accompany an expense. You can in any case get a fair form for around $1,000, or even less on the off chance that you set forth the energy to track down them, yet you might need to work out your spending plan to around $1,200 to represent rising part costs.

The amount Slam do I want for gaming?

The amount Slam you want relies upon what you're hoping to escape your gaming experience. You can get a ton of games with only 8GB of Slam, and 16GB is just about ideal for taking care of even the most in fact requesting titles and projects. You can track down arrangements with 32GB or even up to 128GB of Slam, however in addition to the fact that this extensively expands the expense of the form, but on the other hand it's needless excess. Higher Slam designs are best utilized by imaginative experts delivering 3D workmanship and activity, and for gaming, you begin to see consistent losses after 32GB.

Do I want a devoted GPU to play computer games?

You do, as a matter of fact. Numerous new computer processor chips have some kind of incorporated illustrations handling unit, however it's best utilized for extremely relaxed home utilize like streaming Netflix or checking out at your auntie's get-away photograph collection on Face book. To send off the most well known game titles, you want a committed GPU, however it doesn't need to be an extravagant, costly one. You can utilize a more seasoned card like a GTX 1650 or Radeon RX 5500 regardless get a ton of mileage out of your fabricate.

THE END

www.ingramcontent.com/pod-product-compliance
Lightning Source LLC
LaVergne TN
LVHW051750050326
832903LV00029B/2837